SOLO E♭ ALTO SAX

T0210396

Charlie Parker *with Strings Revisited*

GLENN ZOTTOLA *Alto Sax*

To access audio visit:
www.halleonard.com/mylibrary

Enter Code
1378-3864-9316-5643

ISBN 978-1-94156-695-4

EXCLUSIVELY DISTRIBUTED BY

HAL•LEONARD®

Visit Hal Leonard Online at
www.halleonard.com

Contact Us:
Hal Leonard
7777 West Bluemound Road
Milwaukee, WI 53213
Email: info@halleonard.com

In Europe contact:
Hal Leonard Europe Limited
42 Wigmore Street
Marylebone, London, W1U 2RN
Email: info@halleonardeurope.com

In Australia contact:
Hal Leonard Australia Pty. Ltd.
4 Lentara Court
Cheltenham, Victoria, 3192 Australia
Email: info@halleonard.com.au

Glenn Zottola - Charlie Parker with Strings Revisited

In keeping with the exhaustive body of knowledge – both written and oral - that is the lore of jazz, the classic Charlie Parker with Strings Sessions of 1949 and 1950 provide an enormously abundant amount of both musical and historical content. The impact of these two recording sessions – ones which rate a close second in historical impact to Louis Armstrong's classic Hot Five and Hot Seven recordings – would ripple throughout the music industry, its market and the inhabitants of both.

By the late 1940s, Charlie Parker, already legendary and reigning supreme as the "King of Bebop," was already knighted as a musical visionary. His impact in aggressively moving jazz improvisation away from its Swing Era predecessors had already taken a firm grasp on both jazz musicians and music alike. Although he was not classically trained, Parker had a long-time interest in and affection for the classical orchestral presentation - even to the point of the rumored "visiting" Igor Stravinsky and Bird's interest in studying with Edgar Varése. Thus, when fate allowed him to sit in and perform Neal Hefti's "Repetition" at a Carnegie Hall concert in 1947, it instigated and ignited a deeper desire on Parker's part to explore performing with a larger, traditionally classically-oriented ensemble. Producer Norman Granz, then of Mercury Records and relatively new to the game, was originally skeptical of the concept of a jazzer mingling musically with a string accompaniment. Granz feared that the combination would have limited market potential. However, after numerous requests from Bird, Granz realized that, given Parker's magnetic charisma, there just might be additional broad market and commercial appeal to having the jazz giant perform in a combined small jazz group/string ensemble setting.

On November 30, 1949, Parker, excited to fulfill a long-time dream, entered Mercury's New York City studios with a superb rhythm section consisting of pianist Stan Freeman, bassist Ray Brown, and drummer, Buddy Rich. The quartet was backed by a small orchestral string section and with oboist/English hornist extraordinaire, Mitch Miller (by then himself a fledgling recording executive) added. The format was similar to a Baroque *concerto grosso* with Bird's jazz quartet the *concertino* and the orchestra the *ripieno*. They performed a series of well-known popular standards arranged and conducted by Jimmy Carroll (who would eventually develop a long-term working relationship with Miller as a result of the Parker session). The six selections initially released included Parker's biggest hit, "Just Friends," "April in Paris," "If I Should Lose You," and others.

With the commercial success of the November session, Parker returned to the studio on July 5, 1950 for a second standards session with strings, albeit with Bernie Leighton replacing pianist Freeman, Joe Lipman (who was later affiliated with vocalists Sarah Vaughn, Billy Eckstine and Connie Francis) handling the arranging and conducting duties, and with different orchestral personnel. The repertoire which followed the "standards format" of the fall session included "Dancing in the Dark," "Laura," "I'm in the Mood for Love," and others.

The arrangers' task on both of these celebrated sessions was such that the orchestra ensemble would frame Parker in a manner similar to that of accompanying a vocalist. Since both Carroll and Lipman possessed that skill in significant quantity, the charts functioned seamlessly with Parker's presentations.

Bird's performances on the two dates have become legendary for numerous reasons. His playing on these classic sessions had all of the fire and intrigue of his best prior and subsequent small group *oeuvre*. While the Mercury execs Granz and Miller had visions of expanding jazz into a broader market appeal, Parker steered a true, yet highly complementary,

Bebop course. His ability to deliver the complete improvisational integrity and vocabulary of Bebop, while simultaneously allowing the orchestral accompaniment to frame him well speaks not only to Bird's incredible musical artistry, but also to his immediate adaptability to the unique ensemble format. Further, to Mercury's delight, Parker's brilliant embellishment of melody allowed the recordings to appeal to listeners who, while might not having been thoroughly familiar with Bebop, could certainly "approach" Bird's playing without trepidation.

One must also remember that by the time of these recordings the Great American Songbook was already a musically nutritious resource for Beboppers who (primarily to avoid copyright and royalty issues) grabbed onto basic chord structures of tunes such as "I've Got Rhythm," "How High the Moon," "Out of Nowhere" and others and overlaid more exotic and harmonically complex Bebop melodies. Thus, Parker and others in the Bop mold were intimately familiar with this repertoire.

The album's impact was multiple. The two strings recordings were among Bird's best-selling recordings. They also led other jazz musicians – musicians who were always looking to follow their musical Moses to the Bop Promised Land – to explore unique ensemble and textural formats. Those would include the famous Mercury sessions of *Clifford Brown with Strings* – a gloriously performed classic – and the legendary Columbia collaborations of Miles Davis and Gil Evans. Few know that Parker later actually recorded a later aborted strings session with Gil Evans. Many other jazz musicians followed Parker's lead of fronting an orchestral ensemble. Many jazz players eventually sought to in one way or another re-create the Parker with Strings concept albums. Those artists include the late Phil Woods (an adoring acolyte of Parker's who was married to Parker's widow, Chan Richardson Parker and who adopted Parker's daughter), Stan Getz, Chet Baker, Wynton Marsalis and many others. To this extent, the Parker sessions ripple throughout jazz history to the current day.

In 1995, Verve Records released a compilation of the celebrated Mercury sessions, titled *Charlie Parker with Strings: The Master Takes*. It included a number of previously unreleased selections from the Mercury outings, as well as a recording of Parker playing on the Neal Hefti 1947 "Repetition" date.

There's thinking that the 1949-1950 Parker string sessions were a link between Bebop and Pop. An analysis of the pop music of the time will show that, while the Parker Mercury sessions made no effort to hide an interest by the producers to reach a wider market for jazz, leading jazz musicians were already exploring diverse venues – Davis had his "Birth of the Cool," and later Gil Evans collaborations such as their *Porgy and Bess* and *Sketches of Spain* Columbia collaborations. Furthermore, the era of the Bird with Strings sessions was the period before the explosion of R&B, which spawned Rock 'n' Roll. Years later pop artists such as Frank Sinatra, Neil Diamond, Barbra Streisand, Rod Stewart and Tony Bennett would attempt to integrate the orchestral format.

Much has been written about the musical legacy of Charlie Parker. It is conjectured that had he not died at 35 in 1955, Parker, ever the explorer and musical messiah, would have probably ventured deeper into more "exotic" orchestral formats and other unique fare. While his death at an early age was a tragic loss for music, the resonance that Parker's work possesses, as witnessed in the Strings sessions – and as presented here in this outstanding offering by Glenn Zottola – validate the inclusion of the Parker with Strings sessions as acknowledged as one of the most influential jazz recordings of all time. Yes, as long as artists continue to explore and redefine this marvelous art form, Bird does live indeed.

– Nick Mondello

Charlie Parker *with Strings Revisited*

GLENN ZOTTOLA *Alto Sax*

CONTENTS

MMO 12232

SOLO E♭ ALTO SAXOPHONE

Just Friends

music by
John Klenner
lyrics by
Sam M. Lewis

tend - ing_____ it is - n't the end - ing._____ Two

friends, _____ drift-ing a - part. _____ Two friends, _____ one brok - en heart, _____

_____ we loved, we laughed, we cried, and sud - den-ly love

1:01

died, the sto - ry ends and we're just friends.

(ENGLISH HORN)

1:22

friends, _____ lov - ers no

Two friends, _____ drift-ing a - part. _____ Two

friends, _____ one brok - en heart, _____

_____ we loved, we laughed, we cried, and sud - den - ly love

died, the sto - ry ends and we're just friends.

SOLO E♭ ALTO SAXOPHONE

April in Paris

music by
Vernon Duke
lyrics by
E.Y. "Yip" Harburg

MMO 12232

SOLO E♭ ALTO SAXOPHONE

Summertime

music and lyrics by
George Gershwin,
Dubose and Dorothy Heyward
and Ira Gershwin

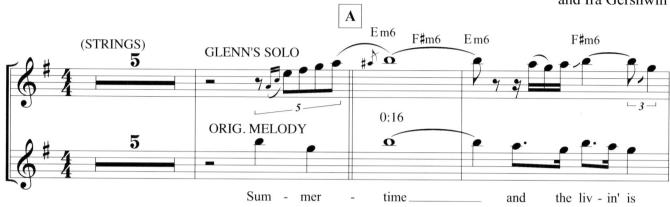

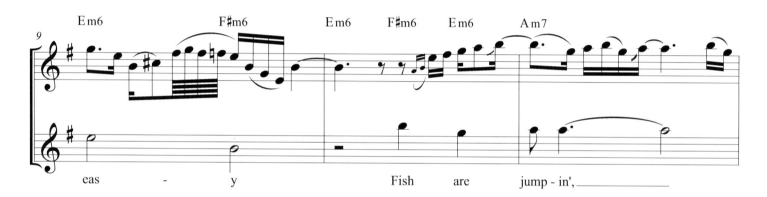

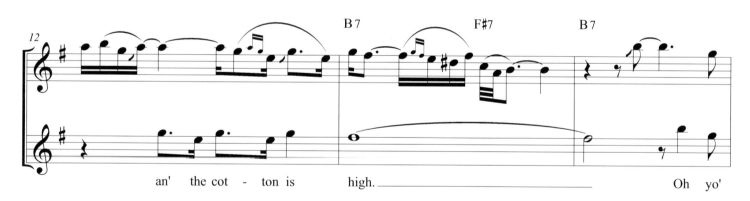

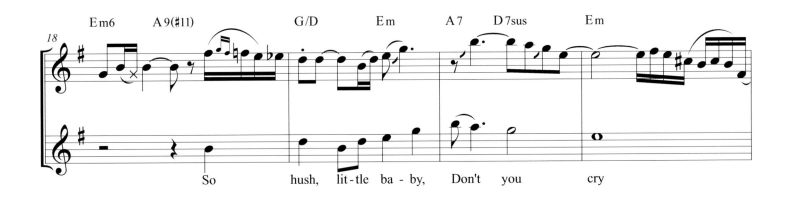

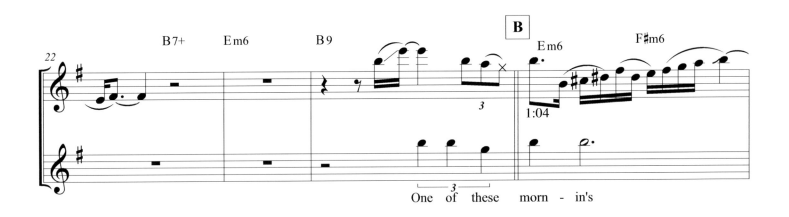

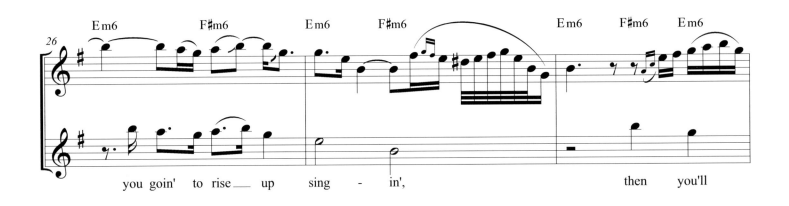

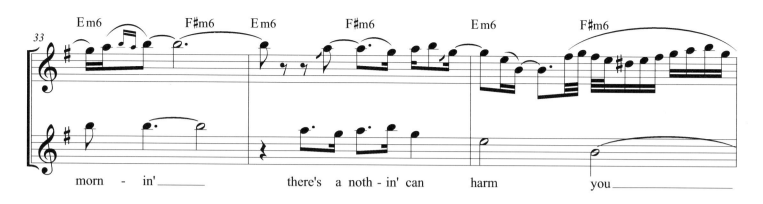

morn - in' _____ there's a noth - in' can harm you _____

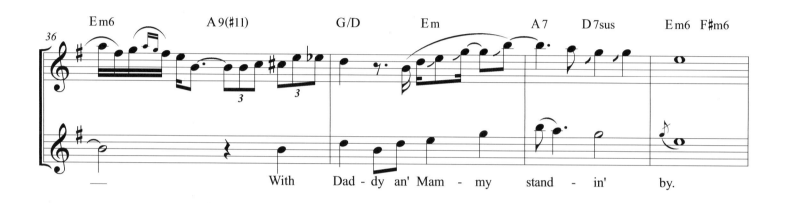

___ With Dad - dy an' Mam - my stand - in' by.

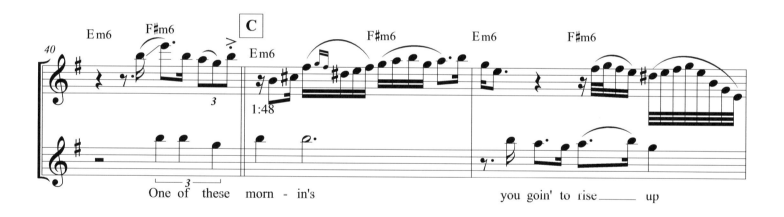

One of these morn - in's you goin' to rise _____ up

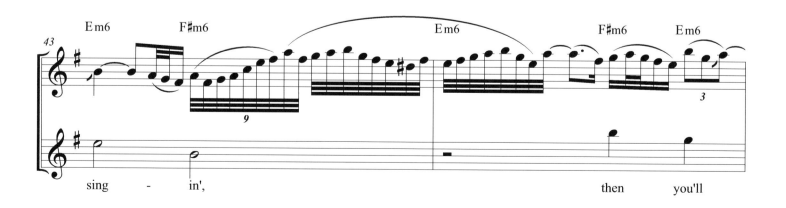

sing - in', then you'll

spread yo' wings an' you'll take the sky. But till that

morn - in' _____ there's a noth - in' can harm you _____

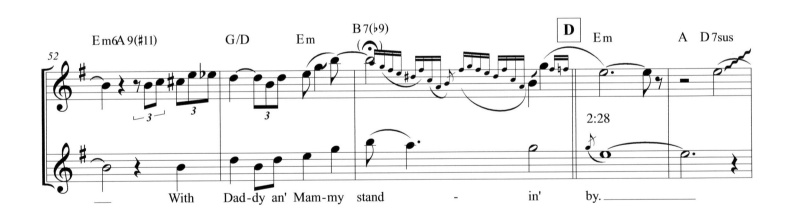

With Dad-dy an' Mam-my stand - in' by. _____

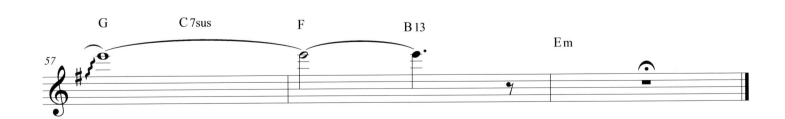

SOLO E♭ ALTO SAXOPHONE

East of the Sun
(and West of the Moon)

music and lyrics by
Brooks Bowman

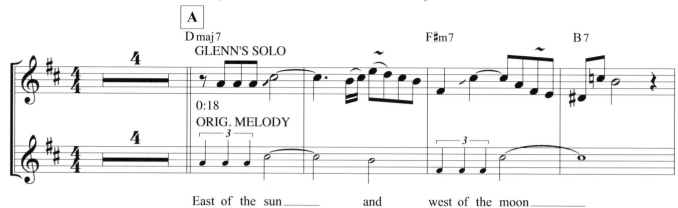

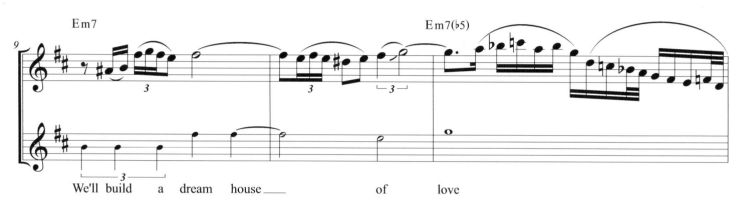

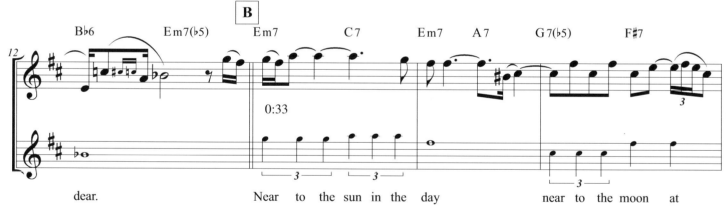

MMO 12232

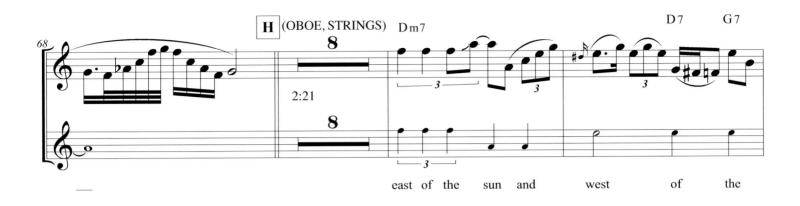

east of the sun and west of the

moon.

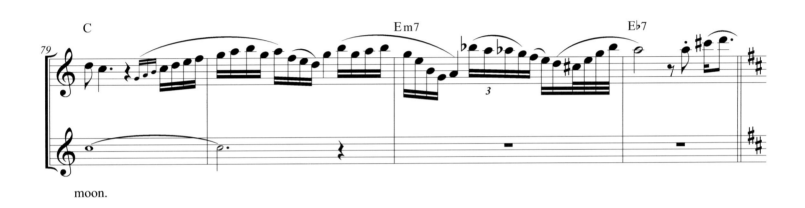

Just you and I _____ for - ev - er and a

day   love will not die, _____ we'll

keep it that way. _____ Up a - mong the

stars we'll find, a har - mo - ny of life to a love - ly tune, east of the sun and

west of the moon dear, east of the sun and

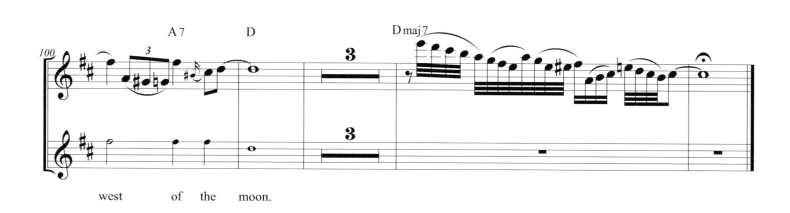

west of the moon.

SOLO E♭ ALTO SAXOPHONE

music by
Richard Rodgers
lyrics by
Lorenz Hart

I Didn't Know What Time It Was

you.   Oh,_____ what a love - ly time it was,

how   sub - lime it was   too.

I_____ did - n't know what day it was. You_____ held my

hand,   warm___ like the month of May it was,   and I'll say it was grand.

(ENGLISH HORN)

2:14

Grand to see your face, feel your touch, hear your voice say I'm all your own.

I did-n't know what year it was, life was no prize.

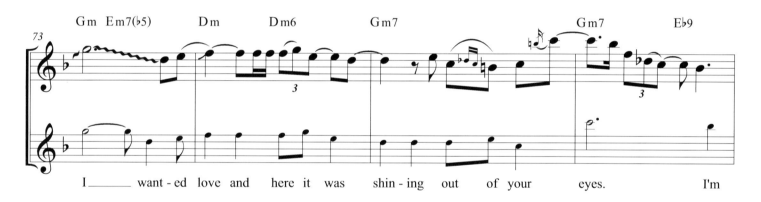

I want-ed love and here it was shin-ing out of your eyes. I'm

wise and I know what time it is now.

SOLO E♭ ALTO SAXOPHONE

Laura

music by
David Raksin
lyrics by
Johnny Mercer

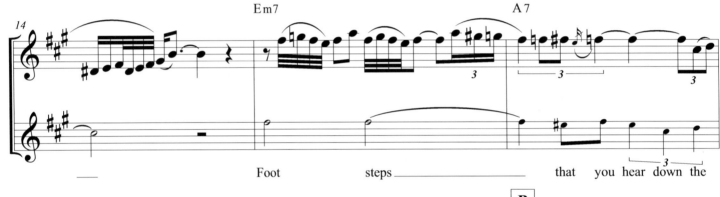

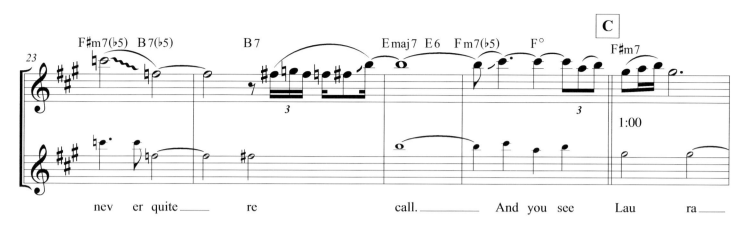

never quite___ re call.___ And you see Lau ra___

___ on the train that is passs ing thru.___

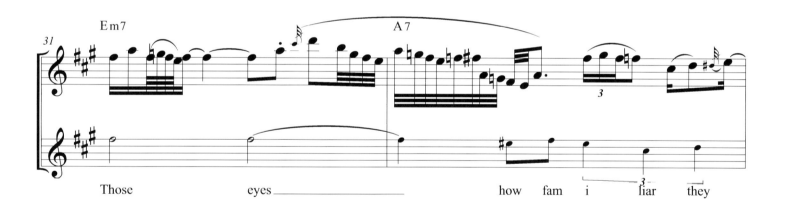

Those eyes___ how fam i liar they

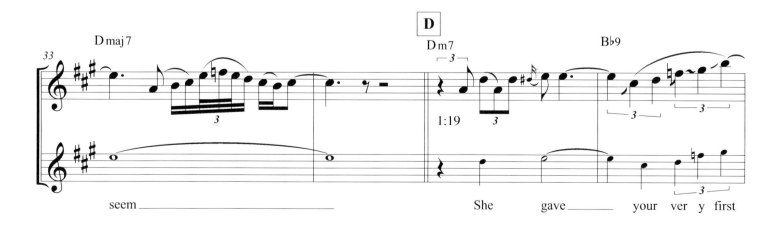

seem___ She gave___ your ver y first

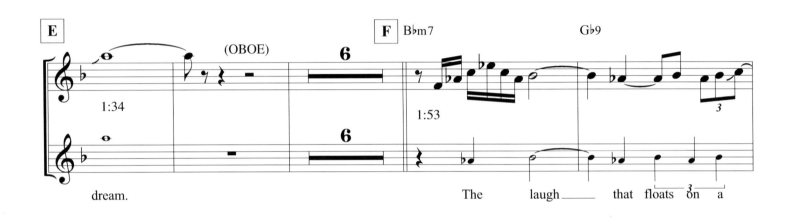

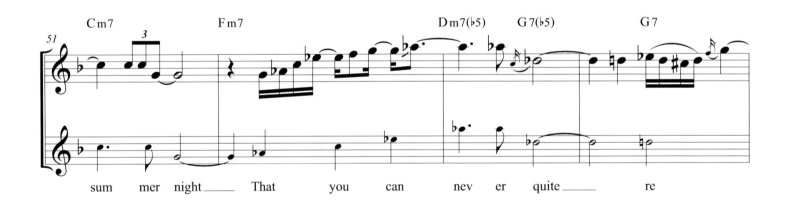

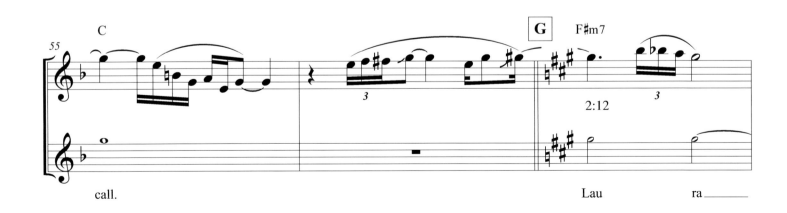

SOLO E♭ ALTO SAXOPHONE

music by
Jimmy McHugh
lyrics by
Dorothy Fields

I'm in the Mood for Love

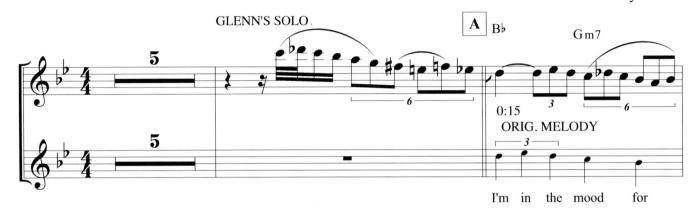

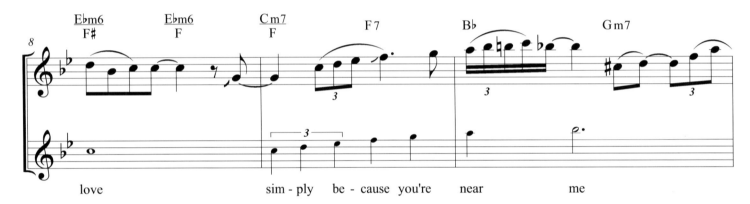

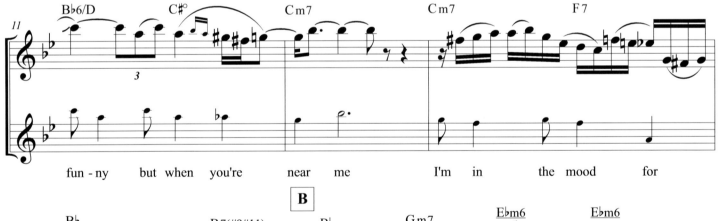

SOLO E♭ ALTO SAXOPHONE

music and lyrics by
Tom Adair and
Matt Dennis

Everything Happens To Me

SOLO E♭ ALTO SAXOPHONE

Dancing in the Dark

music by
Arthur Schwartz
lyrics by
Howard Dietz

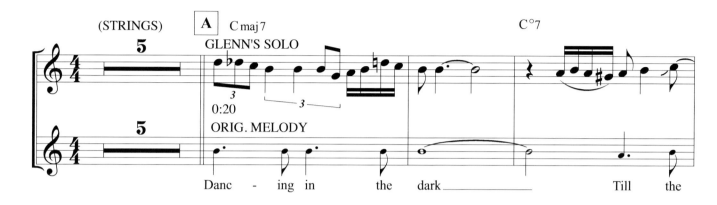

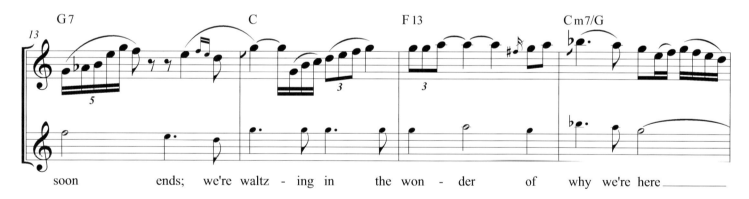

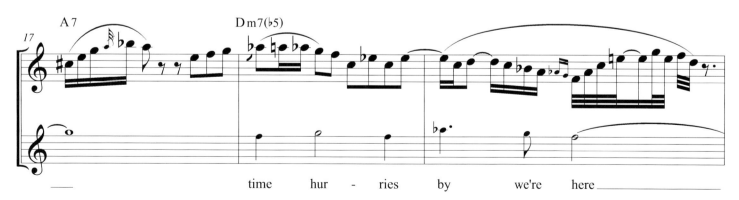

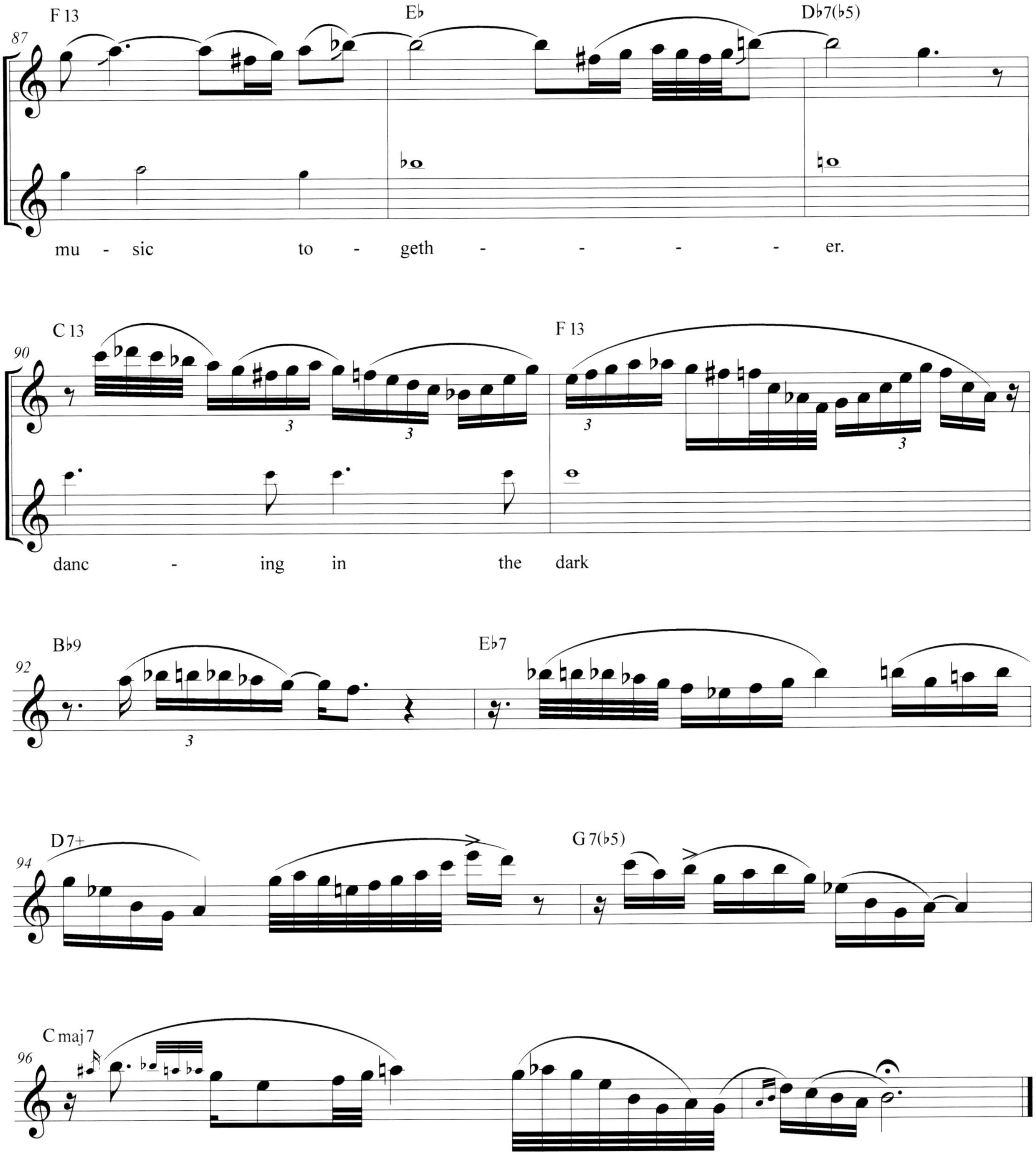
F 13
E♭
D♭7(♭5)
87
mu - sic to - geth - - - - er.
C 13
F 13
90
danc - ing in the dark
B♭9
E♭7
92
D 7+
G 7(♭5)
94
C maj 7
96

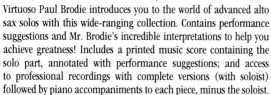

ADVANCED ALTO SAX SOLOS – VOLUME 1

Performed by Paul Brodie, alto saxophone
Accompaniment: Antonin Kubalek, piano

Virtuoso Paul Brodie introduces you to the world of advanced alto sax solos with this wide-ranging collection. Contains performance suggestions and Mr. Brodie's incredible interpretations to help you achieve greatness! Includes a printed music score containing the solo part, annotated with performance suggestions; and access to professional recordings with complete versions (with soloist) followed by piano accompaniments to each piece, minus the soloist. Includes works by Vivaldi, Jacob, Whitney, and Benson.

00400602 Book/Online Audio..............................**$16.99**

ADVANCED ALTO SAX SOLOS – VOLUME 2

Performed by Vincent Abato, alto saxophone
Accompaniment: Harriet Wingreen, piano

Listen as extraordinary virtuoso Vincent Abato of the Metropolitan Opera Orchestra takes you further into the advanced repertoire with these spectacular sax selections. Listen to his masterful interpretations, examine his performance suggestions, then you step in and make magic with Harriet Wingreen, legendary piano accompanist for the New York Philharmonic. Includes: Schubert "The Bee," Rabaud "Solo de Concours," and Creston "Sonata, Op. 19" 2nd and 3rd movements. Includes a printed music score containing the solo part, annotated with performance suggestions; and tracks with complete versions (with soloist) followed by piano accompaniments to each piece, minus the soloist.

00400603 Book/Online Audio **$16.99**

PLAY THE MUSIC OF BURT BACHARACH
ALTO OR TENOR SAXOPHONE

Along with lyricist Hal David, Burt Bacharach penned some of the best pop songs and standards of all time. These superb collections let solo instrumentalists play along with: Alfie • Blue on Blue • Do You Know the Way to San Jose • I Say a Little Prayer • Magic Moments • This Guy's in Love with You • Walk on By • What the World Needs Now • The Windows of the World • and Wives and Lovers.

00400657 Book/Online Audio **$22.99**

BOSSA, BONFÁ & BLACK ORPHEUS FOR TENOR SAXOPHONE – A TRIBUTE TO STAN GETZ
TENOR SAXOPHONE
featuring Glenn Zottola

Original transcriptions for you to perform! The bossa novas that swept the world in 1950 created a whole new set of songs to equal the great standards of the '20s, '30s and '40s by Gershwin, Porter, Arlen, Berlin, Kern and Rodgers. This collection for tenor sax is a tribute to the great Stan Getz and includes: Black Orpheus • Girl from Ipanema • Gentle Rain • One Note Samba • Once I Loved • Dindi • Baubles, Bangles and Beads • Meditation • Triste • I Concentrate on You • Samba de Orfeu.

00124387 Book/Online Audio..............................**$16.99**

CLASSIC STANDARDS FOR ALTO SAXOPHONE
A TRIBUTE TO JOHNNY HODGES
featuring Bob Wilber

Ten classic standards are presented in this book as they were arranged for the Neal Hefti String Orchestra in 1954, including: Yesterdays • Laura • What's New? • Blue Moon • Can't Help Lovin' Dat Man • Embraceable You • Willow Weep for Me • Memories of You • Smoke Gets in Your Eyes • Stardust. Bob Wilber performs the songs on the provided CD on soprano saxophone, although they are translated for alto saxophone.

00131389 Book/Online Audio..............................**$16.99**

EASY JAZZ DUETS FOR 2 ALTO SAXOPHONES AND RHYTHM SECTION

Performed by Hal McKusick, alto saxophone
Accompaniment: The Benny Goodman Rhythm Section:
George Duvivier, bass; Bobby Donaldson, drums

This great collection of jazz duets gives you the opportunity to accompany saxophonist Hal McKusick and the Benny Goodman Rhythm Section. Suitable for beginning players, all the selections are great fun. This album allows you to play either duet part. Includes printed musical score with access to online audio tracks: you hear both parts played in stereo, then each duet is repeated with the first part omitted and then the second part, so you can play along.

00400480 Book/Online Audio..............................**$16.99**

FROM DIXIE TO SWING
CLARINET OR SOPRANO SAX

Performed by Kenny Davern, clarinet
Accompaniment: Kenny Davern, clarinet & soprano sax; 'Doc' Cheatham, trumpet; Vic Dickenson, trombone; Dick Wellstood, piano; George Duvivier, bass; Gus Johnson Jr., drums

Such jazz legends as Dick Wellstood, Alphonse 'Doc' Cheatham and George Duvivier and more back you up in this amazing collection of New York-style Dixieland standards. After the break-up of the big-band era around 1950, many of the finest 'swing' or mainstream players found themselves without an outlet for their abilities and took to playing 'Dixieland' in New York clubs such as Eddie Condon's and the Metropole. And so was born a new style of Dixieland jazz minus the banjos, tubas, steamboats and magnolias! It is this version we celebrate on this album. We encourage you, the soloist, to invent counter-melodies rather than mere harmony parts. This is a music of loose weaving parts, not one of precision ensemble figures. And in short, it is one of the greatest improvisational experiences any jazz player could hope to have. Includes a printed music score and online audio access to stereo accompaniments to each piece.

00400613 Book/Online Audio **$16.99**

GLAZUNOV – CONCERTO IN E-FLAT MAJOR, OP. 109; VON KOCH – CONCERTO IN E-FLAT MAJOR
ALTO SAXOPHONE

Performed by Lawrence Gwozdz, alto saxophone
Accompaniment: Plovdiv Philharmonic Orchestra
Conductor: Nayden Todorov

Alexander Glazunov, one of the great masters of late Russian Romanticism, was fascinated by the saxophone and by jazz. In 1934 he wrote this beautiful saxophone concerto which has become a classic, combining romanticism with modern idioms as well. Erland von Koch's 1958 saxophone concerto is filled with experimental modern tonalities and fantastic effects for the saxophone. Both are must-haves for the serious saxophonist. Includes a printed music score; informative liner notes; and online audio featuring the concerti performed twice: first with soloist, then again with orchestral accompaniment only, minus you, the soloist. The audio is accessed online using the unique code inside each book and can be streamed or downloaded.

00400487 Book/Online Audio **$16.99**

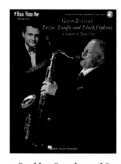